Comptroller of the Currency
Administrator of National Banks

Comptroller's Handbook for Compliance

September 1991

Comptroller's Handbook for Compliance

Table of Contents

Note: Sections of the 1991 handbook that have been replaced by subsequent guidance are not included in this handbook.

The OCC assures that the provision of banking services by national banks is consistent with legal and ethical standards of fairness and corporate citizenship. It performs that obligation by encouraging banks to establish effective compliance management systems and emphasizing that bank management ensure that those systems work. The OCC's approach to promoting compliance and supervising bank compliance management systems in individual banks has two emphases.

First, compliance supervision is essential to overall bank supervision policy. Effective compliance management contributes to the portfolio manager's overall risk assessment in developing the supervisory strategy for each bank and determining the nature and timing of follow-up examination activities.

Second, compliance examinations are conducted to verify the effectiveness of compliance management. The subject currently covered in this handbook is bank securities activities. Procedures for fiduciary (asset management) activities, Community Reinvestment Act (CRA) performance, and compliance with consumer protection, fair lending, and Bank Secrecy Act/anti-money laundering laws can be found in other booklets of the *Comptroller's Handbook* and the *FFIEC BSA/AML Examination Manual*.

Procedures

These compliance examinations use tiered procedures. They are organized in two tiers to focus the examination on the internal control systems implemented by the bank. Some sections may have only Tier I procedures.

Tier I

The Tier I procedures represent a review of controls, policies, and management compliance systems. These procedures are structured to evaluate the existence and quality of management supervision and controls to ensure and monitor compliance with laws and regulations. They include procedures to test or validate selected control functions, to collect information necessary to evaluate the bank's overall conditions, and to support future compliance efforts.

Although Tier I represents the minimum review needed to determine the adequacy of a bank's compliance systems, sufficient examiner discretion and flexibility have been built into the procedures. Flexibility represents the depth or level of testing that the examiner decides is necessary to reach a conclusion for the area being reviewed. To assist in making this decision, the instructions to the compliance procedures suggest that the examiner consider the:

- Adequacy of the audit.
- Other work performed by the bank.
- The applicability of the activity being reviewed to the bank being examined.
- The adequacy of internal controls, including effective policies and procedures.

The examiner should reinforce his or her conclusions about the adequacy of the bank's systems through testing or verification.

Tier II

Tier II procedures are more detailed in coverage and should be used if the examiner is unable to reach a conclusion about a particular area or Tier I procedures reflect significant violations, control deficiencies, and/or other supervisory concerns that warrant the use of additional procedures. The examiner should select only the Tier II procedure(s) considered necessary and appropriate to evaluate the bank's compliance systems. These procedures, or portions thereof, normally would be required only in the absence of sound audit, management, internal controls, and/or insufficient documentation to assess the quality of these functions. Tier II procedures also are useful for training examiners with less experience in a particular area.

Note: Introduction updated August 2007.

Municipal Securities Rulemaking Board (MSRB)

The objective of these procedures is to determine the adequacy of the bank's operating policies and the compliance management systems for the bank's municipal securities and government securities dealer activities. Certain sections of Tier I include elements common to both areas. These sections include board supervision and policies, management supervision, the compliance and audit functions, and compensation. The common elements should not be duplicated. The examiner should assess the work performed by the compliance and audit staffs and minimize duplication if possible. This requires judgmental sampling and decision making by the person performing the procedures. The Appendix provides guidelines to be included and reviewed to determine if the area or system is satisfactory. Certain procedures may be excluded if the bank dealer is not acting in all capacities detailed (e.g., underwriting, sales, and trading). Procedures addressing board and management supervision, audit, compliance management, and compensation should also be used as part of the evaluation of compliance for the bank's government securities activities.

To ensure that examination requirements are satisfied, examiners must at a minimum:

- Complete all of the Tier I examination procedures.
- Document conclusions drawn from these procedures and obtain managerial commitments for appropriate corrective action.
- Send the bank the results of the examiners' conclusions.

Reasons for concluding the supervisory review at the end of Tier I should be documented in a memorandum to the supervisory file.

Based on the pre-examination of the audit or compliance department, the examiner should use a judgmental sample to perform the following procedures. The sample should include new customer accounts; employee; officer and director accounts; personal accounts of employees of other banks; transactions with own or affiliate bank trust accounts; transactions with own or affiliate bank investment portfolios; personal accounts of employees of other securities dealers; underwritings; and the bank's most active and profitable accounts. The sample should be the same as that used by the audit or compliance department. The sample does not have to be the same size as the audit or compliance sample, but the same items should be used.

Review updates of laws and regulations to determine additional examination efforts. Check with the district complaint specialist to determine the number, nature/subject, and resolution of customer complaints about bank securities activities.

Tier I Procedures

Refer to the securities activities section of the Appendix for additional guidance in assessing the bank's policies.

Board of Director Supervision and Securities Underwriting and Trading Policies

1. Assess the adequacy of written securities under-writing/trading policies established by the board of directors or a designated committee by determining whether the policies:

   a. Outline objectives.

   b. Assign responsibility for the supervision and daily operation of dealer activities.

   c. Establish limits and/or guidelines for dealer activities. (Refer to the Appendix for minimum requirements, step 1.)

   d. Address potential conflicts of interest and establish appropriate procedures. (Refer to the Appendix for minimum requirements, step 2.)

   e. State procedures for periodic independent verification and valuation of trading inventories to market value.

   f. Require reporting by department supervisors, compliance managers, and internal auditors to ensure overall compliance with established policies, including MSRB fair practice rules. (Refer to the Appendix, step 3.)

2. Determine whether the dealer department policies are reviewed at least annually by the board or designated committee to determine their adequacy relative to changing conditions.

3. Assess whether the board or board committee, at least annually, ensures that the dealer department is in compliance with its policies.

4. Determine whether possible violations of laws, rules, and regulations are referred to legal counsel for review, and if so, whether counsel submits written opinions to the board or a committee.

Dealer Department Management Supervision

5. Determine whether one or more municipal/government securities principals have been designated as responsible for supervising the activities and business of the dealer, and the activities of its associated people, and if so, note name(s) and area of responsibility. (MSRB Rule G-27.)

6. Determine whether one or more municipal securities principals have been designated as responsible for the maintenance and preservation of books (MSRB Rule G-27) and records required to be maintained by MSRB Rules G-8 and G-9, and if so, note name(s).

7. Determine if written supervisory procedures are in effect that comply with MSRB Rule G-27. (Refer to Appendix. step 9.)

8. Determine if the municipal dealer has conducted an annual review of its supervisory systems and written supervisory procedures to determine that they are adequate and up-to-date. (MSRB Rule G-27(d).)

9. Evaluate management's commitment to correcting matters cited in reports of examination. If matters have not been corrected, determine why (Refer to the Appendix for guidelines, steps 5 through 8.)

10. Determine if all violations, possible violations, or deficiencies that have been reported to the board or designated committee by either the audit staff or compliance staff have been corrected or adequately addressed.

11. Determine whether the dealer department maintains a written customer complaint file. (MSRB Rule G-8 (xii).)

12. Ascertain whether customer complaint follow-up memoranda are prepared, submitted to, and approved by senior managers.

13. Determine whether dealer department employees have written job descriptions.

14. Determine whether the dealer department has a formalized training program.

15. Determine whether the dealer department has records, which include:

    a. Personnel registration and investigation information.

    b. Profit analysis by trader.

    c. Sales production reports.

    d. Account reconcilement and follow up.

    e. Periodic open position reports computed on a trade date or when issued basis.

    f. Reports of own bank credit extensions used to finance the sale of trading account securities.

Compensation

16. Determine the type of compensation program established for the bank's securities dealer employees.

17. If securities dealer employees are compensated pursuant to an incentive compensation program, determine if the program is:

    a. Established in writing.

    b. Approved initially by the board.

    c. Reaffirmed annually thereafter.

    d. Subject to written supervisory procedures (Refer to the Appendix, step 10, and Investment Securities Division (ISD) Notice #3 for minimum guidelines.)

Compliance Management

(This function can be performed by the audit department or the compliance officer.)

18. Determine if the bank has a written compliance policy.

19. Evaluate whether the written policy calls for compliance testing and establishes the following criteria:

    a. Frequency.

    b. Scope.

    c. Timing and method for testing new product compliance.

20. Determine whether a person(s) is responsible for compliance with applicable rules, laws, and regulations and whether that person:

    a. Is independent.

    b. Is qualified (based on training and experience) to monitor effectively the assigned areas.

    c. Performs periodic (at least annual) reviews of all securities dealer activities to determine compliance.

    d. Conducts those reviews pursuant to written compliance testing procedures. (See Appendix for standards, step 13.)

21. Determine if the person responsible for compliance prepares a written dealer compliance report to the board or designated board committee at least annually. (See Appendix, step 12.)

22. Determine if the scope of the compliance review is sufficient to review compliance with laws, rules, regulations, and policy constraints. (Refer to the Appendix for minimum scope, step 12.)

Audit

23. Assess whether the bank's audit staff (either internal or holding company)

periodically reviews the bank's dealer activities, including their compliance with applicable rules and regulations and whether:

a. The department is independent and qualified in this area.

b. The review is conducted at least annually.

24. Evaluate whether comprehensive written audit policies and procedures exist for securities activities, and

a. For new products, determine if prior to their public offering, written audit procedures were developed.

b. If not, ascertain the audit staff's policy for new product development and implementation.

25. Determine if the auditor and/or compliance officer review for MSRB Fair Practice Standards. (See Appendix Fair Practices, steps 14 through 54.)

26. Determine if the audit staff checks for the payment of the annual fee as stated under MSRB Rule A-14.

The following section applies to Municipal Securities Rulemaking Board rules.

Customer Protection

27. Determine if the dealer department maintains on file written customer suitability information and if that information is reviewed as part of the customer account review. If not, determine the reliability of the designated municipal securities principal's MSRB Rule G-27 review of the customer account for suitability, churning, and compliance with customer investment objectives.

NOTE: MSRB Rule G-8(a)(xi) requires documentation of responses to suitability inquiries made pursuant to Rule G-19(b). See narrative discussion of MSRB rules and suitability contained in Section 204.1 of the Comptroller's Handbook for National Bank Examiners. Also see ISD Notice #19 (Appendix).

28. Determine the frequency of the customer account review.

29. Provide the names of the persons conducting the customer account review.

30. Ascertain if a customer account review, required by MSRB Rule G-27(c)(iii), is conducted pursuant to written policies and procedures.

31. Determine whether the review is undertaken by a municipal securities principal with the primary objective of preventing and detecting customer abuse, and if not, why not. (See Appendix, MSRB Rule G-19.)

32. Determine whether the written results of this review are communicated to senior department management and to the board or designated board committee.

33. Determine whether all objectionable or criticized practices cited in the written review have been addressed adequately.

34. Determine if the dealer department maintains and enforces written numerical price markup guidelines. (See narrative discussion of MSRB Rule G-30 contained in Section 204.1 of the *Comptroller's Handbook for National Bank Examiners.*

35. Ascertain if the guidelines also include an "As Agent" fee schedule. (MSRB Rule G-18, "As Agent" Transactions.)

36. Determine whether exceptions to the written price markup or "As Agent" guidelines are reviewed by the person responsible for compliance.

Conclusions

37. Discuss with an appropriate officer:

    a. The soundness of trading objectives, policies, and practices.

    b. The degree of market risk assumed by trading operations.

    c. The effectiveness of analytical, reporting, compliance, and control systems.

    d. Violations of law and their causes.

e. Internal control deficiencies and their underlying causes.

f. Apparent or potential conflicts of interest.

g. Other significant matters.

38. Summarize in a memorandum the results of the Tier I review. Refer to the beginning of this section to determine if all or a portion of Tier II procedures should be performed. The items to be addressed in the memorandum are:

a. Department management.

b. Compliance management.

c. Compliance with law.

d. Internal audit.

e. Condition of the department.

f. Future prospects.

39. Results of the supervisory review, including violations of laws, rules, regulations, or significant deficiencies, and management response should be discussed in the examination report provided to the board of directors. The causes of such violations or deficiencies should be emphasized. Violations and deficiencies found by the examiner and by internal audit and/or compliance management that remain uncorrected should be commented upon.

Tier II Procedures

Registration and Qualification

12 CFR 10, 15 U.S.C. 78o-4(b)(2)(A), (C), and (H) and MSRB Rules G-1 through G-7 — Dealer Registration and Standards of Professional Qualification

1. If the dealer is registered as a separately identifiable department or division, review relevant minutes of the board of directors and determine whether an officer or officers have been designated as responsible for the day-to-day conduct of municipal securities dealer activities.

2. If the dealer is registered as a separately identifiable department or division, review a representative sample of the dealer's records and determine whether those pertaining to municipal securities dealer activities are maintained separately or are extractable from records of the rest of the bank.

3. Review dealer personnel and bank payroll records and determine whether the dealer maintains a current list of all municipal securities principals and representatives, indicating each person's name, residence address and category of function performed, and whether he or she has taken and passed the appropriate MSRB qualification examination or, if not, why not.

4. Obtain an ARRS report from Compliance Management. Review the report and dealer personnel and bank payroll records and determine whether a completed Form MSD-4 has been submitted to the OCC for each municipal securities principal or representative.

   If the municipal securities professional is no longer employed, a completed Form MSD-5 must be submitted.

5. Review job description and background investigation records and associated persons' registration forms (Form MSD-4) to determine if unqualified persons are engaged in municipal securities dealer activities and if the bank dealer has determined if employees are qualified.

6. Review personnel and commission or payroll records and determine whether any municipal securities principal or representative not

previously qualified in a general securities or municipal securities capacity transacted any municipal securities business with the public or received compensation for any municipal securities transaction during the first 90 days of association with the dealer.

7. Review personnel records and, if the dealer has 11 or more employees, determine whether at least two are municipal securities principals. If the dealer has fewer than 11 employees, determine if at least one is principal.

8. If the dealer or any of its municipal securities principals or representatives were disqualified under MSRB rules since the last examination, review commission, production, or sales records for the relevant time period and determine whether any municipal securities transactions were effected by the disqualified person or dealer.

15 U.S.C. 78o-4(b)(2)(J) and MSRB Rules A-12 and A-13 — MSRB Assessments

9. Review correspondence with the MSRB and determine whether the $100 initial fee required by MSRB Rule A-12 has been paid.

10. Review underwriting account records and determine whether the dealer has acted as sole underwriter or as sole or joint manager of a syndicate or similar account acting as underwriter of municipal securities since the last examination. If so, review relevant correspondence files and determine whether the dealer has submitted the underwriting assessment and information on the issue required by MSRB Rule A-13.

Recordkeeping

If the bank dealer uses an automated recordkeeping and/or records maintenance system that can be relied upon to produce timely and accurate records required by MSRB rules G-8 and G-9, the examiner may use discretion about the extent of examination testing. The criteria is:

If the automated system previously has been subject to an OCC review for compliance; and has not undergone substantive modification or redesign since the prior OCC review; and is included as part of the bank dealer's own internal compliance review; and is included as part of the bank's internal audit compliance review; and neither the OCC nor internal reviews previously have resulted in violations of MSRB rules or criticisms of recordkeeping management; then a significant reduction in testing for compliance with MSRB Rules G-8 and G-9 will be permitted at the discretion of the examiner in charge of the MSRB compliance review with the written concurrence of the examiner responsible for the bank compliance examination.

The examiner should document his/her decision in the appropriate work papers.

15 U.S.C. 78o-4(b)(2)(G) and MSRB Rules G-8 and G-9 — Recordkeeping Rules

The MSRB rules do not specify how the municipal securities dealer books and records are to be maintained provided that the information is clear, accurate and provides an adequate basis for audit.

NOTE: A negative response indicates a violation of the rule. Items marked with (**) are not part of the MSRB rule and are only recommended by the OCC. Negative answers to these items will not indicate rule violations.

11. Review recordkeeping systems and test a sample of municipal securities transactions to determine compliance with MSRB Rule G-8. Check to see that the bank maintains:

   a. Order tickets that include:

   - Capacity as principal or agent.

   - Whether order is firm or conditional.

   - Terms, conditions or instructions, and modifications.

   - Type of transaction (purchase or sale).

   - Execution price.

   - Description of security.

   - Date and time of order receipt.

   - Date and time of execution.

- Dealer's or customer's name.

- Delivery and payment instructions.

- Terms, conditions, date, and time of cancellation of an agency order

b. Purchase and sale journals or blotters that include for all purchases and sales:

- Trade date.

- Description of securities.

- Aggregate par value.

- Unit dollar price or yield.

- Aggregate trade price.

- Accrued interest.

- Name of buyer or seller.

- Name of party received from or delivered to.

- Bond or note numbers.

- Indication if securities are in registered form.

- Receipts or disbursements of cash.

- Specific designation of "when issued" transactions.

- Transaction or confirmation numbers recorded in consecutive sequence to ensure that transactions are not omitted. **

- Other references to documents of original entry. **

c. Short sale ledgers that include:

- Sale price. **

- Settlement date.

- Present market value. **

- Basis point spread. **

- Description of collateral. **

- Cost of collateral or cost to acquire collateral. **

- Carrying charges. **

d. Security position ledgers that show separately for each security positioned for the bank's own account:

- Description of the security.

- Posting date (either trade or settlement date, provided posting date is consistent with other records of original entry).

- Aggregate par value.

- Cost.

- Average cost. **

- Location.

- Count differences classified by the date on which they were discovered.

NOTE: For questions dealing with position ledgers, multiple maturities of the same issue of municipal securities and multiple coupons of the same maturity may be shown on same record, provided that adequate secondary records identify such maturities and coupons separately.

e. Securities transfer or validation ledgers that include:

15

- Address where securities were sent.

- Date sent.

- Description of security.

- Aggregate par value.

- Registered securities, containing:

    - Present name of record.
    - New name to be registered.
    - Old certificate or note number.
    - New certificate or note number.
    - Date returned.

f. Journals or tickets for securities received and delivered that include:

- Date of receipt or delivery.

- Name of sender and receiver.

- Description of security.

- Aggregate par value.

- Trade and settlement dates.

- Certificate numbers.

g. Cash or wire transfer receipt and disbursement tickets that include:

- Draft or check numbers.

- Customer accounts debited or credited.

- Notation of the original entry item that initiated the transaction.

h. Cash or wire transfer journals that additionally include:

- Draft or check reconcilements.

- Daily totals of cash debits and credits.

- Daily proofs.

i. Fail ledgers that include:

- Description of security.

- Aggregate par value.

- Price.

- Fail date.

- Customer or dealer name.

- Resolution date.

- A distinction between a customer and a dealer fail.

- Follow-up detail regarding efforts to resolve the fail. **

j. Due bill ledgers that include: **

- Description of securities sold.

- Aggregate par value.

- Price.

- Date of receipt of customer funds.

- Customer name.

- Description of collateral.

- Market value of collateral.

- Date collateral was assigned or deposit reserve treatment commenced.

- Date securities sold were delivered.

k. Securities borrowed and loaned ledgers that include:

- Date of transaction.

- Description of securities.

- Aggregate par value.

- Market value of securities.

- Contra-party name.

- Value at which security was loaned.

- Date returned.

- Description of collateral. **

- Aggregate value of collateral. **

- Market value of collateral. **

- Collateral safekeeping location. **

- Dates of periodic valuations. **

l. Records concerning written or oral put options, guarantees, and repurchase agreements that include:

- Description of the securities.

- Aggregate par value.

- Terms and conditions of the option, agreement, or guarantee.

m. Customer account information that includes:

- Customer's name and residence or principal business address.

- Whether customer is of legal age.

- Occupation.

- Name and address of employer, and whether the customer is employed by a securities broker or dealer or by another municipal securities dealer.

- Name and address of beneficial owner or owners of the account if other than customer and whether:

    - Transactions are confirmed with such owner or owners.

    - The signature of municipal securities representative introducing the account appears.

    - The signature of municipal securities principal accepting the account appears.

- For discretionary accounts:

    - The customer's written authorization to exercise discretionary authority.

    - Written approval of the establishment of such account by the municipal securities principal who supervises the account.

    - Written approval by the supervising municipal securities principal for each transaction in the account, indicating the time and date of approval.

- Name and address of person(s) authorized to transact business for a corporate, partnership or trusteed account and whether:

    - There is a copy of powers of attorney, resolutions, or other evidence of authority to effect transactions for such an account. **

- For borrowing or pledging securities held for the accounts of customers, written authorization from the customer approving such activities. ** (See BC-196)

- Customer complaints that include:

    - Records of all written customer complaints.

    - Record of actions taken concerning those complaints.

n. Customer and the bank dealer's own account ledgers that include:

- All purchases and sales of securities.

- All receipts and deliveries of securities.

- All receipts and disbursements of cash.

- All other charges or credits.

o. Records of syndicates' joint accounts or similar accounts formed for the purchase of municipal securities that include:

- Underwriter agreements, and:

    - A description of the security.

    - The aggregate par value of the security.

- Syndicate or selling group agreements, and:

    - Participants' names and percentages of interest.

    - Terms and conditions governing the formation and operation of the syndicate.

    - Date of closing the syndicate account.

- Reconcilement of syndicate profits and expenses.

- Additional requirements for syndicate or underwriting managers that include:

  - All orders received for the purchase of securities from the syndicate or account, except bid at other than the syndicate price.

  - All allotments of securities and the price at which sold.

  - Date of settlement with the issuer.

  - Date and amount of any good faith deposit made with the issuer.

- A record of all deliveries to purchasers of new issue securities of official statements or other disclosures concerning underwriting arrangements.

p. A record of all designations of persons responsible for the maintenance and preservation of books and records required by MSRB rule G-27.

12. Review record retention systems and test a sample of municipal securities transactions to determine compliance with MSRB Rule G-9.

A negative response to the following indicates a violation of the rule.

a. Check to see if the bank preserves the following municipal securities records for the periods of time indicated:

- An itemized daily record of all purchases and sales, all receipts and deliveries of securities, all receipts and disbursements of cash, and all other debits and credits pertaining to municipal securities for six years.

- Customer and bank dealer's own account ledgers for six years.

- Customer complaint records for six years.

- Customer account information relating to the opening and

maintenance of the account for a period of at least six years following the closing of an account.

- Securities position ledgers for six years.

- Records of syndicate transactions for six years. (Such records need not be preserved for an account that was unsuccessful in purchasing an issue of municipal securities.)

- Records of each person designated as responsible for the maintenance and preservation of banks and records for six years.

- Secondary records for three years that include:

  - Transfer, validation, borrowed or loaned, and fail ledgers or tickets.

  - Put options and repurchase agreements.

  - Records of principal and agency transactions (order tickets and confirmations).

  - Checkbooks, checking account statements, cancelled checks, reconcilements, and wire transfers.

  - Receivables and payables.

  - All written communication received or sent, including interoffice memoranda, on the conduct of activities in municipal securities transactions.

  - All other customer account information.

  - All other written agreements entered into for any municipal securities account.

b. Determine if all records are required to be kept in a readily accessible place for at least two years, and thereafter in a reasonably accessible place.

c. If records are kept in any manner other than in the original format of the record, determine if the bank has facilities for ready retrieval, inspection, and reproduction of legible facsimiles.

Underwriting

15 U.S.C. 78o-4(b)(2)(K) and MSRB Rule G-11 — Sales of New Issue Municipal Securities During the Underwriting Period

13. Review all syndicate participations and transactions with related portfolios and determine if sales of syndicate securities to related portfolios were effected.

    If so, review confirmations from syndicate managers to determine if the manager confirmed the sale for the account of the related portfolio on the basis of disclosures made by the bank dealer under examination.

14. For syndicates where the dealer bank is the manager, review priority provisions, written communications, and the disclosure of allocation of securities and syndicate expenses.

Negative responses for the following indicate violations of the MSRB Rule G-8 — Records of Syndicate Transactions.

15. Determine if there are records of syndicates' joint account or similar accounts formed for the purchase of municipal securities that include:

    a. Underwriter agreements and:

        • A description of the security.

        • The aggregate par value of the issue.

    b. Syndicate agreements of the selling group, indicating:

        • Participants' names and percentages of interest.

        • Terms and conditions governing the formation and operation of the syndicate.

        • Date of closing of the syndicate account.

23

- Reconcilement of syndicate profits and expenses.

16. Determine if there are additional records for syndicate or underwriting managers that include:

   a. All orders received for the purchase of securities from the syndicate or account, except bids at other than the syndicate price.

   b. All allotments of securities and the price at which they are sold.

   c. Date of settlement with the issuer.

   d. Date and amount of any good faith deposit made with the issuer.

17. Review complaints filed by other municipal securities dealers about the bank's underwriting activities and determine the validity of those complaints and compliance with all provisions of G-11.

18. Determine if the bank purchased/sold any securities to/from an affiliate, who was the principal underwriter, without the approval of a majority of the directors who are not bank officers or employees. (Federal Reserve Act section 23B) (12 U.S.C. 371c).

Confirmations

If the bank dealer uses an automated system to produce dealer (MSRB Rule G-12) and customer (MSRB Rule G-15) securities transaction confirmations and the automated system can be relied upon to produce timely and accurate transaction confirmations, the examiner may use discretion about the extent of examination testing. The criteria are as follows: If the automated system previously has been subject to an OCC review for compliance; and has not undergone substantive modification or redesign since the prior OCC review; and is included as part of the bank dealer's own internal compliance review; and is included as part of the bank dealer's internal audit compliance review; and neither the OCC nor the internal reviews previously resulted in violations of MSRB rules or criticisms of securities transaction confirmation practices; then a significant reduction in testing for compliance with MSRB rules G-12 and G-15 will be permitted at the discretion of the examiner in charge of the MSRB compliance review with the written concurrence of the examiner responsible for the bank compliance examination.

The examiner should document his/her decision in the appropriate work papers.

15 U.S.C 78o-4(b)(2)(C) and MSRB Rule G-12 — Uniform Practice

19. Review appropriate municipal securities records and operational systems and test a sample of transactions that involve other municipal securities brokers or dealers, and:

   a. Determine if "regular way" dealer confirmations are sent within one business day following the trade date.

   b. Determine if initial "when, as and if issued" (WI) dealer confirmations are sent within two business days of trade date and if final WI confirmations are sent to nonsyndicate members at least five business days before settlement date.

   c. From sample items, determine if the information included on dealer confirmations conforms to the requirements of MSRB Rule G-12.

Negative responses indicate violations of the rule.

20. Determine if dealer confirmations include, when applicable (required by MSRB rule G-12):

   a. Bank dealer's name, address and telephone number.

   b. Contra-party identification.

   c. Designation of purchase from or sale to.

   d. Par value of securities.

   e. Description of securities, including at a minimum:

      • Name of issuer.

      • Interest rate.

      • Maturity date.

- Designation, if securities are limited tax.

- Subject to redemption prior to maturity (callable).

- Designation, if revenue bonds and the type of revenue.

- The name of any company or person in addition to the issuer, who is obligated, directly or indirectly, to pay debt service on revenue bonds. In the case of more than one such obligor, the phrase "multiple obligors" will suffice.

- Dated date, if it affects price or interest calculations.

- First interest payment date, if other than semiannual.

- Designation, if securities are "fully registered" or "registered as principal."

- Designation, if securities are "pre-refunded."

- Designation, if securities have been "called," maturity date fixed by call notice, and amount of call price.

- Denominations of bearer bonds, if other than denominations of $1,000 and $5,000 par value up to $100,000 par value.

- Denomination of registered bonds, if other than multiples of $1,000 par value up to $100,000 par value.

- Denominations of municipal notes.

f. CUSIP number, if assigned.

g. Trade date.

h. Settlement date.

i. Yield to maturity and resulting dollar price. Only the dollar price need be shown for securities traded at par or on a dollar basis. Check to see if:

- For transactions in callable securities effected on a yield basis, the resulting price is calculated to the lowest of price to call premium, par option (callable at par) or to maturity.

- The fact that securities are priced to premium call or par option must be stated, and the call or option date and price used in the calculation, if applicable, must be shown.

j. The amount of concession, if any.

k. Amount of accrued interest.

l. Extended principal amount.

m. Total dollar amount of transaction.

n. Payment and delivery instructions.

o. Special instructions, such as:

- "Ex-legal" (traded without legal opinion).

- "Flat" (traded without interest).

- "In default" as to principal or interest.

21. From confirmation comparison systems, telephone logs, or memoranda, and failure-to-confirm notices and non-recognition notices received, determine if incoming dealer confirmations are compared and verified upon receipt and if discrepancies exist, whether such information is promptly communicated to the contra-party.

22. From failure-to-confirm notices sent and telephone logs or memoranda, determine if the bank dealer recognized a contra-party's failure to confirm or to send a non-recognition notice within four business days after trade date and promptly communicated that information to the contra-party.

23. From copies of non-recognition and failure-to-confirm notices sent, determine if their contents conform to the requirements of MSRB Rule G-

12 (refer to narrative text).

24. From systems for delivery of municipal securities or receipted delivery tickets received, determine if duplicate delivery tickets containing the information required by MSRB Rule G-12 (refer to narrative text in section 204 of The Comptroller's Handbook for National Bank Examiners) accompany delivery of municipal securities.

25. From accrued interest calculation systems and test sample items, determine if accrued interest is calculated to, but not including, the settlement date.

26. From notices of close out received from purchasers and explanations offered in written responses, determine the veracity of such responses by comparing the ones involving offsetting fails-to-receive, items in transit to the purchaser, or sent for transfer, deregistration or validation to appropriate municipal securities ledgers, journals, or tickets maintained by the bank dealer under examination. Written explanations concerning lost or mutilated certificates, coupons, or documentation and requested replacements should be compared to supporting correspondence maintained by the bank dealer.

27. From telephone logs or memoranda on purchaser's telephonic notice of close out, determine if the bank dealer responded within one business day following receipt of a purchaser's notice of close out.

28. From retransmittals of purchasers' closeout notices, determine if the bank dealer retransmitted such notices no later than one business day preceding the date for close out as specified in the original closeout notices, and if the bank dealer attaches a memorandum to each retransmitted purchaser's closeout notice, specifying the extended date for close out resulting from such retransmittal.

29. From telephone logs or memoranda, and written retransmittal responses, determine if the dealer immediately notifies the purchaser, who originates the closeout notice, of the extended date, and if retransmittal responses are made promptly.

30. From notices of close out sent to sellers and telephone logs or memoranda, determine if notices were given not earlier than the fifth business day after the settlement date and if written closeout notices sent

to sellers were accompanied by a copy of the seller's confirmation of the transaction which is the subject of the closeout notice.

31. From closeout notices sent to purchasers, rejection notices received from purchasers, telephone logs and memoranda, determine if the seller's notice of close out was given to the purchaser no later than the close of business on the delivery date.

32. From executions of close out, determine if the transaction was closed out not earlier than the business date following the date telephonic notice of close out was given to the purchaser.

33. If the bank dealer managed syndicates or similar accounts formed to purchase municipal securities from an issuer, review documentation concerning settlement of syndicate transactions and determine if good faith deposits were returned to syndicated members within two business days following settlement with the issuer or in the case of a syndicate which was not successful in purchasing an issue, within two business days following return of the deposit from the issuer.

34. Determine if final settlement of the syndicate was made within 60 days following the date that all securities had been delivered by the bank dealer to syndicate members.

35. If the bank dealer reports the purchase or sale of securities at a given price, compare that price to purchase and sales journals or blotters to determine the report's accuracy.

15 U.S.C. 78o-4(b)(2)(C) and MSRB Rule G-15 — Customer Confirmations

36. Review operational systems and test a sample of transactions in municipal securities involving customers and:

   a. From operational systems, determine if confirmations are sent to customers at or before completion of a municipal securities transaction.

   b. From sample items, determine if the information included on customer confirmations conforms to the requirements of MSRB Rule G-15.

Negative responses for the following indicate violations of the rule.

37. Determine if customer confirmations include, when applicable (required by MSRB Rule G-15):

a. Bank dealer's name, address and telephone number.

b. Customer's name.

c. Designation of whether the transaction was a purchase from or sale to the customer.

d. Par value of securities.

e. Description of securities, including at a minimum:

- Name of issuer.

- Interest rate.

- Maturity rate.

- Designation, if securities are limited tax.

- Subject to redemption prior to maturity (callable).

- Designation, if revenue bonds and the type of revenue.

- The name of any company or person in addition to the issuer who is obligated, directly or indirectly, to pay debt service on revenue bonds. In the case of more than one such obligor, the phrase "multiple obligors" will suffice.)

- Dated date, if it affects price or interest calculations.

- First interest payment date, if other than semiannual.

- Designation, if the securities are available only in book-entry form.

- Designation, if the securities sold are identified as subject to federal taxation.

- Designation, if securities are "pre-refunded".

- Designation, if securities have been "called," maturity date fixed by call notice, and amount of call price.

- Denominations of bearer bonds, if other than denominations of $1,000 and $5,000 par value.

- Denominations of registered bonds, if other than multiples of $1,000 par value up to $100,000 par value.

- Denominations of municipal notes.

- CUSIP number, if assigned.

f. Trade date and time of execution, or a statement that the time of execution will be furnished upon written request of the customer.

g. Settlement date.

h. Yield and dollar price. Only the dollar price need be shown for securities traded at par. Check to see if:

- For transactions effected on a yield basis, the yield and dollar price is shown as calculated to the lowest of price to call, price to par option, or price to maturity.

- For transactions effected on the basis of dollar price, the dollar price as well as the lowest resulting yield to call, yield to par, or yield to maturity is shown.

i. Amount of accrued interest.

j. Extended principal amount.

k. Total dollar amount of transaction.

l. The capacity in which the bank dealer effected the transaction:

- As principal for own account.

- As agent for customer.

- As agent for a person other than the customer.

- As agent for both the customer and another person (dual agent).

m. If a transaction is effected as agent for the customer or as dual agent:

- Either the name of the contra-party or a statement that the information will be furnished upon request.

- The source and amount of any commission or other remunerations to the bank dealer.

n. Payment and delivery instructions.

Special instructions, such as:

- "Ex-legal" (traded without legal opinion).

- "Flat" (traded without interest).

- "In default" as to principal or interest.

38. Review customer correspondence and complaints to determine if requests for information, concerning the identity of contra-parties on agency transactions or the time of execution on any transaction, are answered within five business days following receipt of such requests. In the case of a transaction executed more than 30 calendar days prior to the receipt of such a request, determine if the request is answered within 15 business days.

Fair Practice

15 U.S.C. 78o-4(b)(2)(C) and MSRB Rule G-13 — Quotations Relating to Municipal Securities, and MSRB Rule G-14 — Reports of Sales or Purchases

39. Review advertisements and customer correspondence and complaints about municipal securities to determine if bids for, or offers of securities, are made at prices that relate reasonably to those accepted by the bank

dealer under examination in immediately prior and subsequent trades in the same security.

40. If the bank dealer reports the purchase or sale of securities at a given price, compare that price to purchase and sales journals or blotters to determine the reports' accuracy.

Conclusions

41. Summarize the results of the Tier I and Tier II review in a memorandum and forward a copy to the Investment Securities Division. Items to be addresses are:

    a. Department management.

    b. Compliance management.

    c. Compliance with law.

    d. Internal audit.

    e. Condition of the department.

    f. Future prospects.

42. Results of the supervisory review, including violations of laws, rules, regulations, or significant deficiencies and management response should be discussed in the examination report provided to the board of directors. The causes of such violations or deficiencies should be emphasized. Violations and significant deficiencies found by the examiner and by internal audit and/or compliance management that remain uncorrected should be commented upon.

MSRB and Government Securities Appendix

Tier I Procedures

Board of Director Supervision and Securities Underwriting and Trading Policies

1. The following topics should be included specifically (as applicable) in the bank's policy addressing securities dealer limits and guidelines (Tier I, question 1c). Determine whether the bank's securities dealer policy considers:

   a. Price markups.

   b. Quality of issues.

   c. Maturity of issues.

   d. Inventory position limits, including intra-day position limits, overnight position limits, and WI position limits.

   e. Security types.

   f. Amounts of unrealized loss on inventory positions.

   g. Length of time an issue will be carried in inventory.

   h. Dollar amounts of individual trades or underwriter interests.

   i. Acceptability of brokers and syndicate partners.

   j. New product development (puts and calls, etc.).

   k. Private placements.

2. The following topics should be included specifically (as applicable) in the bank's policy addressing potential conflicts of interest situations. Proper monitoring procedures should also be implemented (refer to question 1d of Tier I). Determine whether the bank's policies and procedures address:

a. Deposit and service relationships with municipalities whose issues have underwriting links to the trading department.

b. Deposit relationships with securities firms handling significant volumes of agency transactions or syndicate participations.

c. Transfers made between trading account inventory and investment portfolio(s).

d. Transactions by officers, directors, or employees of the bank and its affiliates.

e. The bank's trust department acting as trustee, paying agent, and transfer agent for issues that have an underwriting relationship with the trading department.

3. Check to see that the bank's policies specifically address compliance with MSRB rules of fair practice by:

a. Prohibiting any deceptive, dishonest, or unfair practice.

b. Adopting formal suitability checklists.

c. Establishing a system to monitor gifts and gratuities.

d. Establishing a system to ensure that materially false or misleading advertisements are not allowed.

e. Providing for the disclosure and consents necessary to avoid conflicts of interest when the bank assumes the role of both underwriter and financial advisor to the issuer.

f. Adopting a system to determine the existence of possible control relationships.

g. Establishing a system to ensure that confidential, non-public information is not used without prior written approval of the affected parties.

h. Establishing a system to detect the improper use of funds held on another's behalf.

i. Designating a specific principal to supervise personnel and general business conduct.

j. Adopting written securities' price markup guidelines.

k. Allocating responsibility for transactions with own employees (not specifically required by MSRB rules) and employees of other dealers.

l. Requiring the maintenance of the MSRB manual at each office where there are representatives.

m. Requiring disclosure on all new issues.

4. Determine if the bank's policies address applicable government securities activities, including:

   a. Compliance with the Government Securities Act of 1986.

   b. Compliance with 12 CFR 12, including:

      • Supervisory responsibilities.

      • Fair allocation of securities and prices to accounts when orders are simultaneously received and executed.

      • Crossing of buy and sell orders on an equitable basis.

      • Reporting of investment transactions by officers and employees who make investment recommendations or decisions for customer accounts, or obtain information on securities being purchased/sold or recommended for purchase/sale.

   c. Compliance with Banking Circular 210 regarding repurchase transactions.

Dealer Department Management Supervision (BC-228)

5. Review the bank dealer registration form MSD Schedule A and MSD-4 forms to determine if employees:

a. Have a history of rapid job turnover within the securities industry and the reasons for such turnover.

b. Have been associated with firms that have been the subject of disciplinary action.

c. Have been associated with firms that have a poor reputation for integrity.

6. Determine whether all prior violations of laws, rules, and regulations cited in previous supervisory reviews have been corrected.

7. Determine whether all objectionable or criticized practices cited in previous supervisory reviews have been adequately addressed.

8. Determine whether internal control weaknesses cited in previous supervisory reviews have been adequately addressed.

9. Determine whether written supervisory procedures exist, that:

a. Designate one or more municipal securities principals to supervise its municipal securities business and the activities of its associated people, including activities under MSRB Rule G-27(a) and G-27(c).

b. Assign responsibilities and provide for:

- Supervising, maintaining, and preserving books and records.

- Monitoring compliance with all applicable rules.

- Handling customer complaints.

- Reviewing the municipal activities of each office of the dealer.

- Approving the opening of each customer account.

- Reviewing and approving each transaction in municipal securities daily.

- Reviewing and approving all correspondence pertaining to the solicitation or execution of transactions in municipal securities.

c. Provide for the regular and frequent examination and approval of customer accounts by the designated municipal securities principal to detect and prevent irregularities and abuses. Determine:

- If such a review is conducted.

- If it is documented.

- How frequently it is conducted.

- Who conducts it.

Compensation

10. The following supervisory procedures are the minimum that should be included in the review of the bank's incentive compensation program. Check to see whether the procedures require:

a. A review of internal management reports that detail:

- The source and amount of production credits or dollars earned.

- Dollars paid.

- Total dollars deferred for each affected employee.

b. An exception reporting system providing for the timely identification and review of high volume customer accounts and unusually high profit transactions.

c. A mechanism for reporting the actual dollar amounts paid to highly compensated employees.

Compliance Independence

11. Determine whether the person responsible for the dealer department compliance review:

a. Receives compensation that is not based upon profits generated from securities sales.

b. Remains independent of dealer department management and sales incentive compensation.

Compliance Report

12. Ascertain whether the written compliance report includes the:

   a. Scope of the compliance review.

   b. Analysis of which violations and exceptions occurred and why.

   c. Corrective action taken by management.

Dealer Compliance Review

Determine if the following applicable laws, rules, and regulations are reviewed as part of the documented municipal securities dealer department annual compliance review or internal audit department review. If the following are not included in the bank's own compliance or internal audit review, the examiner must document the deficiency, obtain assurance of correction, and perform the applicable steps under the appropriate subject headings in Tier II.

13. Determine whether the scope of the compliance review includes:

   a. Each MSRB rule and U.S. Government Securities Act requirement.

   b. All appropriate SEC rules.

   c. 12 U.S.C. 84 and BC-196 — Borrowed and Loaned Securities.

   d. 12 CFR 1.

   e. 12 CFR 9.12 — Purchase of securities involving fiduciary funds.

   f. 12 CFR 10.

   g. 12 CFR 18 and 12 CFR 11 — Securities Exchange Act Disclosure Rules.

h. 17 CFR 240.17f-1 — Lost and Stolen Securities Program.

NOTE: Coordinate with the person assigned to perform the Commercial Activities — Regulatory Reports procedures.

i. 31 CFR 103 — Bank Secrecy Act.

NOTE: Coordinate with the person assigned to perform the Bank Secrecy Act procedures.

j. 12 U.S.C. 371(c) and 12 U.S.C. 375 — Preferential Treatment.

k. 12 CFR 204 and BC-182 — Due Bills.

l. Review of new products.

m. Customer complaints.

Fair Practice Standards

Except when specifically noted by an asterisk (*), a negative response to any item indicates a violation of an MSRB rule.

15 U.S.C. 78o-4(b) and MSRB Rule G-26 — Customer Account Transfers

14. Determine whether written municipal securities customer account broker-to-broker transfers are coordinated so that:

a. Upon receipt of a customer transfer instruction, the receiving party immediately submits the instruction to the carrying party.

b. The customer account carrying party within five business days validates and returns the instruction or takes exception to and advises the receiving party.

c. The customer account carrying party, within five business days of the validation, completes the transfer of the customer account.

d. The customer account receiving and carrying parties establish fail-to-receive and fail-to-deliver contracts on their books and institute the close-out procedures of MSRB Rule G-12.

15 U.S.C. 78o-4(b) and MSRB Rule G-27 — Supervision

15. Review selected transactions, compliance reviews, policies and procedures and determine if supervision and approval meet the requirements of MSRB Rule G-27.

15 U.S.C. 78o-4(b) and MSRB Rule G-28 — Transactions with Employees and Partners of Other Municipal Securities Professionals

16. Determine if the bank has accounts for anyone employed by, or who is partner of, another municipal securities dealer or on the behalf of any spouse or minor child of such person and if so, whether:

    a. Written notice of the opening and maintenance of such account has been given first to the broker or dealer by whom such person is employed.

    b. The bank sent a confirmation notice to the employing dealer at the same time the notice was sent to the customer at the time of effecting a transaction.

    c. The bank acted according to any written instructions that may have been provided by the employing dealer or broker.

15 U.S.C. 78o-4(b) and MSRB Rule G-29 — Maintenance of Rules

17. Ascertain whether the bank maintains a complete updated copy of all MSRB rules in each office in which any municipal security dealer activities are conducted.

15 U.S.C. 78o-4(b) and MSRB Rule G-32 — Disclosure in Connection with New Issues

18. Review selected transactions and determine if the dealer at or prior to final confirmation sent to the customer information on new issue securities required by MSRB Rule G-32 (records are required per MSRB Rule G-8(a)(xiii)), including:

    a. A copy of the official statement furnished on behalf of the issuer. (If an official statement is not being prepared by an issuer, the dealer must

41

provide written notice to that effect.)

b. For a negotiated sale of a new issue, whether the following information was delivered to the customer:

- The underwriting spread.

- The amount of any fee received by the municipal securities dealer as agent for the issuer in the distribution of the securities.

- The initial offering price for each maturity in the issue that is offered or to be offered in whole or in part by the underwriters.

NOTE: The above requirements must be met at or prior to the sending of the final confirmation notice.

15 U.S.C. 78o-4(b) and MSRB Rule G-21 — Advertising

19. Review department advertising of services and securities and determine if:

a. Copies of all professional and product advertisements are maintained in a separate file.

b. The advertisement contains information that is not materially false or misleading. Refer to ISD notice #16.

c. Dated principal approval is indicated on all advertisements prior to "first use."

20. Determine if advertisements of a new issue of securities contain the information required by MSRB Rule G-21.

21. Determine if the bank has advertised any new issues of securities, or part thereof, showing the initial reoffering prices or yields for the securities, even if the price or yield for a maturity or maturities may have changed. If so, ascertain whether the advertisements:

a. Contain the date of sale of the securities by the issuer to the syndicate.

b. Show either the initial reoffering prices or yields or the prices or yields that existed at the time the advertisement was placed for publication.

15 U.S.C. 78o-4(b) and MSRB Rule G-18 — Execution of Transactions

22. Determine whether the bank dealer uses the proper criteria in determining if its capacity in a transaction is that of principal or agent by reviewing policies and procedures and through discussions with sales personnel.

23. Test selected transactions and:

    a. From agency transactions, determine if a reasonable effort (i.e., obtaining three or more quotes) was made to obtain a price for the customer that is fair and reasonable relative to prevailing market conditions.

    b. Determine if the same reasonable effort was made to obtain a fair and reasonable price for "broker's" broker transactions.

15 U.S.C. 78j and MSRB Rule G-19 — Suitability of Recommendations and Transactions (See also Banking Circular 228)

24. Review selected customer files to determine if all information required by MSRB Rule G-8(a)(xi) is obtained at or before completion of a transaction.

25. Review selected customer files to determine if all appropriate information (financial background, tax status, investment objectives, etc.) was obtained and retained (see MSRB Rule G-8(a)(xi)) and based on this information, determine if:

    a. The dealer has reasonable grounds to believe that the recommendation is suitable for that customer.

    b. The dealer has no reasonable grounds to believe that the recommendation is unsuitable for that customer.

    c. Any transaction effected that the dealer believed to be unsuitable for that customer, after informing him/her in writing of same, was done only at the customer's direction.

    d. The size and frequency of transactions indicates customer account churning.

15 U.S.C. 78o-4(b) and MSRB Rule G-20 — Gifts and Gratuities

26.Review policies and procedures, compliance reviews, internal audit review, customer complaints, expense records, minutes of meetings and determine if the dealer directly or indirectly permits gifts or gratuities in excess of $100 per year. *

15 U.S.C. 78o-4(C) and MSRB Rule G-22 — Control Relationships

27.Review department personnel files or any other records to determine if:

a. Any control relationships exist.

b. Any transaction was effected by a dealer with a control relationship without first disclosing the relationship before entering into a contract, and if such disclosure is not made in writing that it was supplemented by written disclosure at or before the completion of the transaction.

15 U S.C. 78o-4(b) and MSRB Rule G-23 — Activities of Financial Advisors

28.Review financial advisory relationships and determine if:

a. Each relationship is evidenced by a written agreement entered into prior to, upon, or promptly after the inception of the financial advisory relationship.

b. Such written agreement sets forth the basis of compensation for services rendered, including provisions relating to the deposit of funds or the use of fiduciary or agency services.

29.Compare the listing of underwritings since the last examination to the listing of financial advisory relationships. Identify situations in which the bank dealer acted as financial advisor and underwriter for the same issuer. For those issues underwritten on a negotiated basis, determine if:

a. The financial advisory relationship was terminated in writing.

b. The bank dealer obtained express written consent from the issuer to acquire the securities on a negotiated basis.

c. The bank dealer expressly disclosed in writing to the issuer, at or before termination of the financial advisory relationship, a possible conflict of interest in changing from financial advisor to negotiated basis purchaser, and the issuer has expressly acknowledged receipt of such disclosures in writing.

   d. The bank dealer has expressly disclosed in writing to the issuer, at or before termination of the financial advisory relationship, the source and anticipated amount of all remuneration.

30. For issues sold by the issuer at competitive bid, determine if the issuer has consented expressly in writing prior to the bid of such bank dealer's acquisition or participation.

31. For affected securities, determine if appropriate customer disclosures have been made in writing to customers at or before completion of the transaction.

32. Determine whether copies of written documents, notifications, disclosures, etc., as required by MSRB Rule G-9 are being maintained and preserved in accordance with that rule.

15 U.S.C. 78o-4(b) and MSRB Rule G-24 — Use of Ownership Information Obtained in Fiduciary or Agency Capacity

33. Review "buy-back" and larger profit trades and question department personnel to determine if the bank, acting in an agency capacity for other dealers or issuers, has used any confidential, nonpublic information accessible to it through its agent capacity to solicit purchases, sales or exchanges, or for financial gain without specific written approval from one of the affected parties. A prohibited data source would include the bank's trust division. *

15 U.S.C. 78o-4(b) and MSRB Rule G-25 — Improper Use of Assets

34. Review customer correspondence and confirmations to determine if the bank has guaranteed or made an offer to guarantee a customer against a loss in a municipal securities transaction. *

35. Review purchase and sales ledgers and determine if the bank has shared in the profits or losses of customer municipal securities transactions. *

15 U.S.C. 78o-4(b) and MSRB Rule G-30 — Prices and Commissions (Refer to pricing in Section 204.1 of the Comptroller's Handbook for National Bank Examiners.)

36. Review customer and inventory records to determine if a dealer has effected any principal transactions that were not at a fair and reasonable price (blotters and trade tickets, etc.). *

37. Review customer records and income journals to determine if the bank, while functioning in an agency capacity, has effected any transactions for commissions or service charges that exceed a fair and reasonable amount. *

15 U.S.C. 78o-4(b) and MSRB Rule G-17 — Conduct of Municipal Securities Business

38. Based on the review of prior items and the bank's own internal review, determine if it has engaged in any deceptive, dishonest, or unfair practice. *

12 CFR 12 — Recordkeeping and Confirmation Requirements for Securities Transactions (Refer to Government Securities Procedures)

39. Test for compliance by answering Internal Control questions 37 through 48 in the Investment Securities section 203.4 of the Comptroller's Handbook for National Bank Examiners.

12 CFR 1.3 — Eligible Securities

40. Review inventory schedules of underwriting and trading accounts to determine if the par value of issues exceed the 10 percent limit of 12 CFR 1.

41. Verify that the total par value of Type II obligations does not exceed the 10 percent limit of 12 CFR 1 when combined with holdings in the bank's investment portfolio.

12 CFR 11 — Securities Exchange Act Disclosure and
12 CFR 18 — Reports to Shareholders

42. Verify that the bank's trading account inventory and trading income are

reported appropriately.

12 U.S.C. 371c and 12 U.S.C. 375 — Preferential Treatment

43. Determine whether transactions, including securities clearance services, with affiliates, directors, and officers and their related business interests, are on terms less favorable to the bank than transactions involving unrelated parties.

12 CFR 9.12 — Purchase of Securities Involving Fiduciary Funds

44. Review customer accounts and determine if trading or underwriting securities were purchased with funds held by the bank in a fiduciary capacity.

12 CFR 204.2 and BC-182 — Due Bills

45. Review outstanding due bills and determine if (see steps 11 and 12 of GSA Tier I for due bills involving U.S. Government obligations):

   a. The customer was provided full and written disclosure of all material facts.

   b. Safekeeping receipts are sent to safekeeping customers only after the purchased security has been delivered.

   c. Due bills are issued only in those instances in which the bank, despite a diligent good faith effort, is unable to deliver the securities purchased by the customer.

   d. In the absence of a diligent good faith effort, demand deposit reserves are maintained from the date of receipt of customer funds, and that the customer is informed of the bank's intent to obtain the securities.

   e. Due bills outstanding over three business days are collateralized or properly reserved.

   f. Collateralized due bills are secured by securities of the same type and of comparable maturity and with a market value at least equal to the security that is the subject of the due bill.

12 U.S.C. 84 and BC-196 — Borrowed and Loaned Securities

46. Review a list of borrowed and loaned securities and determine if the collateral pledged is composed of securities similar to and having a market value at least equal to the loaned or borrowed securities.

15 U.S.C. 78j — Unsafe and Unsound Practices and Possible Violations

47. Review customer account schedules of own bank and affiliated bank permanent portfolios, trusts, other broker/dealers, employees of own or other banks, and other broker/dealers. Use an appropriate sampling technique to select transactions and compare trade prices to independently established market prices as of the date of trade.

48. Review transactions, including U.S. government tender offer subscription files, involving employees and directors of own or other banks and determine if the funds used in the transactions were misused bank funds or the proceeds of reciprocal or preferential loans. *

49. Review sales to affiliated companies to determine whether the sold securities were not subsequently repurchased at an additional markup and that gains were not recognized a second time.

50. Review commercial paper sales journals or confirmations to determine if the bank sells affiliate commercial paper. If so, determine whether:

   a. The bank engages in affiliate-issued commercial paper only "as agent" and with sophisticated investors.

   b. Transactions are denominated generally in amounts of $25,000 or more.

   c. Each transaction confirmation clearly discloses that the affiliate-issued commercial paper is not a deposit and is not insured by the Federal Deposit Insurance Corporation.

51. Review securities position records and customer ledgers for large volume repetitive purchase and sales transactions and:

   a. Independently test market prices of significant transactions that involve the purchase and resale of the same security to the same or related parties.

b. Investigate the purchase of large blocks of securities from dealer firms just prior to month end and their subsequent resale to the same firm after the beginning of the next month.

52. Select a representative sample of customer accounts opened during the last three months and determine:

a. The percentage of the total number of selected accounts that involve customers located outside of the bank's service area.

b. The manner in which the new customers' names were selected for solicitation.

c. The type of information on file concerning inquiry into the customers' financial condition and investment needs.

d. Whether initial trades for new customers were executed at market price by comparing trade prices to independently established market prices.

53. Review lists of approved dealer firms and determine whether the approval of any firm that handles a significant volume of agency transactions is based on competitive factors rather than deposit relationships.

54. Review customer complaint files and determine the reasons for such complaints.

ISD Notices #3 and #19

ISD Notice #3 — Compensation — Some dealer banks give their sales representatives a percentage of the profits in the transaction. The OCC does not prohibit compensation based on transactional profit. However, this type of compensation program must be properly approved, managed, and controlled.

ISD Notice #19 — Amendment to MSRB Rule G-8(a)(xi) — Customer Protection — This amendment requires documentation of responses to suitability inquiries made pursuant to G-19(b) which includes information concerning the customer's financial background, tax status, investment objectives, and any other information used or considered to be necessary by bank dealers in making recommendations to customers. The amendment should help enforce the customer protection principles embodied in MSRB Rules G-19 and G-27.

These are the initial examination procedures for dealer banks' government securities activities. All procedures for Tier I must be used for the first two government securities compliance examinations.

Evaluation of the bank's government securities activities should include reviews of board and management supervision, audit, compliance management, and compensation. Specific questions for each of these areas are detailed in the MSRB section, Tier I, and the same questions should be used when evaluating government securities activities. Complete the evaluation by performing the procedures detailed later in this section. The procedures are designed so that negative responses indicate violations of the regulations.

Introduction

This section incorporates the applicable laws and regulations of the Government Securities Act of 1986 (GSA). Section 3(a)(42) of the Securities Exchange Act of 1934 (15 U.S.C. 78c(a)(42)) defines government securities. They include U.S. Treasury securities, federal agencies (issued or guaranteed), and those of government related corporations, such as GNMA, FNMA, FHLMC, Sallie Mae, and Farm Credit. "Off exchange" puts, calls, straddles, and "similar privileges" on government securities also fit the definition.

The GSA directed the Secretary of Treasury to write rules to regulate government securities brokers and dealers. These rules are divided into four functional areas: financial responsibility, investor protection, recordkeeping, and reporting and auditing. National banks are exempt from the financial responsibility requirements of the regulations because they are subject to OCC capital requirements. They are also exempt from the reporting and auditing requirements. The investor protection section regulates repurchase agreement transactions and "due bills," and establishes safeguards over customer-owned securities. The recordkeeping sections of the regulations require banks to keep current records and preserve specific records relating to their securities activities.

Certain provisions of the Government Securities Act of 1986 are not limited to national bank broker/dealer activities. Provisions of the Act also apply to national banks that retain custody of customer securities (hold-in-custody repos), while engaging in repurchase transactions, and national banks that hold government securities for customers.

NOTE: Trust departments must also comply if the bank has not adopted written policies and procedures governing custodial holdings. (As applicable, banks are required to comply with 17 CFR 403.5(d)(1) governing "hold-in-custody" repurchase transactions, and 17 CFR 450 governing custodial holdings of customer securities.

The following summary is provided to assist the examiner in the registration and repurchase agreement requirements of the regulations.

Registration Exemptions

Most banks acting as government securities brokers and/or dealers are required to file with the OCC a form known as a G-FIN. This form details the bank's capacity, the locations where government securities activities are performed, and the persons responsible for supervision. However, certain bank government securities activities are exempt from the filing requirements. Banks handling only U.S. Savings Bond transactions or submitting tender offers on original issue U.S. Treasury securities are exempt from registration.

Limited government securities brokerage activities are also exempt from registration under certain circumstances. Banks effecting fewer than 500 government securities transactions annually (excluding savings bond transactions and Treasury tender offers) are exempt. Similarly, the bank is exempt if it effects transactions with a registered broker/dealer under a "networking" arrangement. However, those banks will be exempted only if they meet the following requirements: (1) the transacting broker must be clearly identified; (2) bank employees perform only clerical or ministerial duties and do not receive transaction-based compensation; and (3) the registered broker dealer receives and maintains all required information for each customer.

Finally, banks may perform limited government securities dealer activities and be exempted from the registration requirements. The bank is exempt if its activities are limited to purchases and sales in a fiduciary capacity and/or purchases and sales of repurchase or reverse repurchase agreements.

The preceding exemptions provide relief from registration, but exempt banks must comply (if applicable) with regulations addressing custodial holdings for customers (17 CFR 450). Additionally, banks effecting repurchase/reverse repurchase agreements must also comply with repurchase transaction requirements detailed in 17 CFR 403.5(d).

Pooling Of Securities

The regulations do not permit pooling of securities that are subject to repurchase transactions. Pooled repurchase transactions occur when a dealer does not identify specific securities as belonging to specific counterparties. Instead, the dealer sets aside or otherwise designates a pool of securities to collateralize its outstanding repurchase transactions. The main concern with pool repurchase transactions is whether they effectively convey an enforceable security interest to the counterparties to the transaction. Previous operational practice with those transactions has been to issue a confirmation that referred only to "various securities." The regulations require that a dealer confirm specific securities to its counterparty in a hold-in-custody transaction. (17 CFR 403.5(d)(1)(ii))

Required Repurchase Agreement Disclosure

When the bank has been granted the right to substitute securities in repurchase transactions, the following disclosure must be included in the written repurchase agreement immediately preceding the provision governing the right to substitution:

"The (seller) is not permitted to substitute other securities for those subject to this agreement and therefore must keep the (buyer's) securities segregated at all times, unless in this agreement the (buyer) grants the (seller) the right to substitute other securities. If the (buyer) grants the right to substitute, this means that the (buyer's) securities will likely be commingled with the (seller's) own securities during the trading day. The (buyer) is advised that, during any trading day that the (buyer's) securities are commingled with the (seller's) securities, they may be subject to liens granted by the (seller) to third parties and may be used by the (seller) for deliveries on other securities transactions. Whenever the securities are commingled, the (seller's) ability to resegregate substitute securities for the (buyer) will be subject to the (seller's) ability to satisfy any lien or to obtain substitute securities."

Confirmation Tickets For Repurchase Agreements

If the bank retains custody of securities or retains the right to substitute securities during a repurchase agreement, it must identify in writing the specific securities that are collateralizing the repurchase agreement. This identification is satisfied by providing the counterparty with a confirmation ticket at the end of day the transaction is initiated. An additional confirmation ticket must be sent out at the end of each day that other securities are substituted by the bank during the repurchase agreement. Only the security involved in the last substitution of the day must be disclosed on the confirmation ticket (17 CFR 403.5(d)(1)(ii)). The confirmation ticket must specify at a minimum the issuer of the security, maturity date, coupon rate, par amount and market value of the security, and the CUSIP or mortgage pool number of the underlying security (17 CFR 403.5(d)(2)(i)).

Tier I Procedures

Registration and Qualification

Registration (17 CFR 400)

National banks acting as government securities brokers and/or dealers are required to "notify" the OCC of the capacity in which they are acting. "Notification" is accomplished by completing and filing a Form G-FIN with the OCC. (15 U.S.C. 78o-5(b)) (17 CFR 400.1(d))

1. Determine if the bank has filed Form G-FIN with the OCC.

2. Ascertain whether the bank has filed an amended Form G-FIN with the OCC if the information contained in it or in any of its amendments is inaccurate. (17 CFR 400.5(b))

Professional Qualifications

Associated Persons (17 CFR 400)

3. Determine whether a Form G-FIN-4 has been submitted to the OCC within 10 days of the person's association with the bank and whether the bank maintains current and complete copies on file. (17 CFR 400.4(d)(1)) (17 CFR 400.4(a))

NOTE: Form G-FIN-4 is not required if the bank maintains a completed and current Form MSD-4 or Form U-4 for the associated person. However, the bank must still notify the OCC that the associated person is registered.

4. Ascertain whether the bank has verified the accuracy of associated persons' Form G-FIN-4 by making inquiries of all previous employers during the preceding three years and by: (17 CFR 400.4(c))

   a. Determining the adequacy of the bank's procedures for ensuring that information detailed by the associated person on Form G-FIN-4 is accurate.

   b. Determining the adequacy of the bank's procedures for ensuring that associated persons correct information which is materially inaccurate or incomplete on the G-FIN-4, MSD-4, or Form U-4.

5. Determine if the bank submits a G-FIN-5, Form MSD-5, or Form U-5 within 30 days of termination, for each associated person whose association has been terminated. (17 CFR 400.4(d)(2))

6. Ascertain whether the bank has submitted a list to the OCC detailing all associated persons who have filed either a Form MSD-4 or Form U-4, and which form has been filed for each. (17 CFR 400.4(d)(1))

7. Determine whether the bank has established procedures to ensure that the information contained in Form G-FIN-4 and Form G-FIN-5 is maintained for at least three years after the person ceases to be associated with the bank's dealer function. (17 CFR 404.4(b)(2))

Investor Protection

Custody of Customer-Owned Securities (17 CFR 403.5)

8. Determine whether the bank has established adequate written procedures and internal controls to determine, on each business day, the quantity and issue of such securities, if any, that are required to be, but are not, in the financial institution's possession or control. (17 CFR 403.5(c)(2))

9. Ascertain whether the procedures address:

a. Releases of liens, charges, or encumbrances against affected securities.

b. Returns of securities loaned.

c. Steps to obtain possession or control of securities failed to receive for more than 30 days (except for mortgage-backed securities).

d. "Buying in" securities as necessary when securities shortages in possession or control cannot be resolved by any of the preceding procedures.

Repurchase Agreements (Hold-In-Custody Repos)

10.If the bank retains custody of securities that are the subject of a repurchase transaction or if the bank retains custody of such securities, whether or not in safekeeping, and retains the right to substitute other securities for such securities, determine whether:

a. The bank ensures that repurchase agreements are in written form. If so, ascertain whether the written repurchase agreement explicitly advises the counterparty that funds held by the bank pursuant to the repurchase agreement are not a deposit and therefore not insured by the FDIC.

b. The bank confirms in writing, at the end of the trading day on which the transaction occurred, the specific securities that are the subject of the transaction. (17 CFR 403.5(d)(1)(ii))

c. The bank maintains possession or control of securities that are the subject of the agreement. (17 CFR 403.5(d)(1)(vi))

d. The bank substitutes collateral resulting in a change in issuer, maturity date, par amount, or coupon rate.

e. If the bank substitutes collateral:

- The bank's right to substitute securities and proper disclosure to the counterparty is included in the written repurchase agreement. (17 CFR 403.5(d)(1)(v))

- The substitution is confirmed in writing with the counterparty at the end of the trading day on which the substitution occurs. (17 CFR 403.5(d)(1)(i))

- The written confirmation provides the customer with adequate disclosure. (17 CFR 403.5(d)(2)(i)) (Refer to the introduction for minimum requirements.)

Due Bills

11. If the bank has accepted customer funds for securities purchases, but has not placed the order by the close of the next business day after receipt, determine whether:

a. The bank immediately deposits or redeposits the funds in the customer's account and sends the customer notice of such deposit and redeposit.

b. If not, the bank complies with the "buy-in" provisions of the regulations.

12. Ascertain whether the bank complies with Banking Circular 182 when issuing "due bills" to customers.

Recordkeeping (17 CFR 404.4)

Bank Broker/Dealer Records

13. Determine whether the bank's securities records or ledgers separately reflect, as of the settlement date:

a. All "long" positions (including securities that are the subjects of repurchase and reverse repurchase agreements) carried by the bank for:

- Its own account.

- For the accounts of its customers or others (excluding securities held in a fiduciary capacity).

b. All "short" positions (including securities that are the subjects of repurchase and reverse repurchase agreements) carried by the bank for:

- Its own account.

- For the accounts of its customers or others (excluding securities held in a fiduciary capacity).

c. The location of all government securities "long."

d. The offsetting position to all government securities "short."

e. "Long" security count differences.

f. "Short" security count differences.

g. The inclusion in security count difference records of:

- The date of the count and verification in which the discrepancies were discovered.

- The name or designation of the account in which each position is carried.

14. Verify that the bank established procedures to ensure that securities records are retained in accordance with retention requirements.

NOTE: The records must be maintained for not less than six years with the first two years of records in an easily accessible place. (17 CFR 450.4(f))

15. Verify that the government securities area has established policies and procedures to comply with the requirements of 31 CFR 103. (Coordinate with the examiner assigned to review Bank Secrecy Act Activities.)

Custodial Holdings of Government Securities (17 CFR 450)

The bank is exempt from the requirements of section 450 if the responses to questions 16 and 17 are yes (17 CFR 450.3). If the bank maintains custody of securities that are not subject to examination for compliance with 12 CFR 9 (e.g., commercial bank safekeeping), the bank must comply with Section 450.

Customer Holdings Subject to Fiduciary Standards

16. Determine whether the bank exercises fiduciary powers.

17. Ascertain if the bank's custodial holdings of government securities:

   a. Are administered pursuant to written policies and procedures that apply all the applicable requirements imposed by the OCC on fiduciary holdings of government securities.

   b. Are subject to examination by the OCC for compliance with such fiduciary requirements.

Customer-Owned Securities Maintained On-Site (17 CFR 450.4)

18. Ascertain whether, if the bank is not exempt and maintains custody of securities on its premises, government securities held for customers are segregated from the bank's assets and kept free from liens of any third party or the bank.

Customer-Owned Securities Maintained at a Third Party (17 CFR 450.4)

NOTE: The bank is not required to have a segregated account at the FED for customer-owned securities if the securities are segregated in the bank's records.

19. Determine whether, if the bank maintains customer-owned securities at a third party:

   a. The bank has notified the third party institution that such securities are customer-owned securities.

   b. The customer-owned securities are maintained in an account specifically designated for bank customers that does not contain securities belonging to the bank.

   c. The bank has instructed the third party to maintain such securities free from liens of the third party or any persons claiming through it.

   d. If the customer-owned securities are maintained by the bank at the FED, any liens or claims granted to FED or any person claiming through the FED expressly exclude customer securities.

Recordkeeping for Custodial Holdings (17 CFR 450.4)

The following recordkeeping requirements DO NOT apply to repurchase transactions (RPs). RPs are addressed in Section 403.5(d). However, these requirements apply to all national banks that hold securities for the account of customers, not only dealer banks. These procedures also are included in GSA Tier I for Non-Dealer Bank Activities.

Recordkeeping

20. Determine whether the bank issues a safekeeping receipt or confirmation for each security held for customers.

21. Determine if the safekeeping receipt or confirmation identifies the:

   a. Issuer.

   b. Maturity date.

   c. Par amount.

   d. Coupon rate.

22. Ascertain whether the bank's records of government securities held for customers are kept separate and distinct from other bank records.

23. Determine if the bank's records:

   a. Identify each customer.

   b. Identify each government security held for each customer (or the amount of each issue issued in book-entry form).

   c. Describe the customer's interest in the security.

   d. Indicate all receipts and deliveries of securities and receipts and disbursements of cash.

   e. Include a copy of the safekeeping receipt or confirmation issued for each government security held.

24. Determine whether the bank's records provide an adequate basis for audit of recordkeeping information.

25. Ascertain whether the bank has established procedures to ensure that government securities held for customers in definitive and book entry form are counted at least annually and that such counts are also reconciled to customer account records.

   NOTE: The regulations require that all government securities held for customers be counted annually. A sample is not acceptable.

26. Determine whether the bank's procedures include verifying securities:

   a. In transfer.

   b. In transit.

   c. Pledged.

   d. Loaned.

   e. Borrowed.

   f. Deposited.

   g. Failed to receive.

   h. Failed to deliver.

   i. Subject to repurchase agreement.

   j. Subject to reverse repurchase agreement.

   k. Subject to the bank's control or direction, but not in its physical possession for longer than 30 days.

27. Determine whether the bank has developed procedures to document the dates and results of such counts and reconciliations and whether they are adequate.

28. Ascertain if differences are noted in a security count difference account

not later than seven business days after the date of each required count and verification.

29. Ascertain whether the bank has established procedures to comply with record retention requirements. The requirements are the same as those for bank broker/dealer recordkeeping.

Securities Lending — Customer-Owned Securities

Securities Lending Practices

30. Determine whether the bank lends customer-owned securities.

31. If the bank lends customer-owned securities, ascertain if it has obtained written authorization from the customer.

32. Determine whether securities lending activities fully comply with Banking Circular 196.

Recordkeeping and Confirmation Requirements

National banks that effect securities transactions for customers are required to comply with the recordkeeping and confirmation requirements of 12 CFR 12. Ignore any exemptions in the regulation for U.S. government securities. The regulation is being amended to accommodate the Government Securities Act.

Securities Records

33. Determine whether the bank maintains "blotters" or other chronological records of original entry, containing an itemized daily record of all purchases and sales of government securities.

34. Ascertain if the chronological records include:

   a. The customer or account for whom the transaction was effected.

   b. Description of the securities.

   c. The unit and aggregate purchase or sale price.

   d. The trade date.

e. The name of the broker/dealer or person from whom purchased or to whom sold.

35. Determine whether the bank maintains account records for each customer that reflect:

    a. All purchases and sales of securities.

    b. All receipts and deliveries of securities.

    c. All receipts and disbursements of cash.

    d. All other debits and credits pertaining to government securities transactions.

Broker/Dealer Commissions

36. Verify that the bank maintains a record of all broker/ dealers used to effect securities transactions (trading area only), including the amount of commissions paid or allocated to each broker/dealer during the calendar year.

Order Tickets

37. Determine whether the bank maintains a separate memorandum of each order to purchase or sell government securities that includes:

    a. The account(s) for which the transaction was effected.

    b. Whether the transaction was a market order limit order, or subject to special instructions.

    c. The time the order was received by the person responsible for effecting the transaction.

    d. The time the order was placed with the broker/dealer, or if no broker/dealer, the time the order was executed or cancelled.

    e. The price at which the order was executed.

f. The broker/dealer used (if applicable).

Customer Notification

38. Ascertain whether, if the bank receives remuneration from the customer or any other source and the remuneration is not determined pursuant to a written agreement between the bank and the customer, the bank provides the customer with a statement of the source and amount of any remuneration to be received.

39. Determine whether the bank provides the customer with a copy of the broker/dealer confirmation relating to the securities transaction.

40. If the bank does not provide the customer with a copy of the broker/dealer confirmation, determine if it furnishes him or her with a written notification that includes:

   a. The bank's name.

   b. The bank's capacity.

   c. The customer's name.

   d. The date of execution.

   e. A statement that the time of execution will be furnished upon the customer's written request.

   f. The description and price of securities purchased/sold.

   g. The name of the broker/dealer used and the amount of commissions received in connection with the transaction.

   h. The source and amount of any remuneration received by the bank in connection with the transaction.

41. Assess the adequacy of procedures established by the bank to ensure that affected customers are notified of securities transactions in a timely manner.

Conclusions

42. Summarize in a memorandum the results of the supervisory review, addressing:

   a. Department management.

   b. Compliance management.

   c. Compliance with law.

   d. Internal audit.

   e. Condition of the department.

   f. Future prospects.

43. Results of the supervisory review, including violations of laws, rules, regulations, or significant deficiencies and management response should be discussed in the examination report provided to the board of directors. The causes of such violations or deficiencies should be emphasized. Violations and significant deficiencies found by the examiner and by internal audit and/or compliance management that remain uncorrected should be commented upon.

Government Securities Act Non-Dealer Bank Activities

Introduction

Certain provisions of the Government Securities Act of 1986 also apply to national banks that are not brokers and/or dealers. Provisions also pertain to national banks that retain custody of customer securities (hold-in-custody repos), while engaging in repurchase transactions, and those who hold government securities for customers. The section of the regulation that addresses "due bills" may also apply to banks acting "as-agent" when effecting securities transactions for customers. Trust departments must also comply if the bank has not adopted written policies and procedures governing custodial holdings. Banks that engage in repurchase transactions without retaining custody of customer securities are not subject to GSA requirements. However, these banks must comply with Banking Circular 210.

This section incorporates the applicable laws and regulations of the Government Securities Act of 1986 (GSA). Section 3(a)(42) of the Securities Exchange Act of 1934 (15 U.S.C. 78c(a)(42)) defines government securities. These securities include U.S. Treasury securities, federal agencies (issued or guaranteed), and those of government related corporations, such as GNMA, FNMA, FHLMC, Sallie Mae, and Farm Credit. "Off exchange" puts, calls, straddles, and "similar privileges" on government securities also fit the definition.

These procedures must be performed only in banks that do not have dealer departments. There are no Tier II procedures for this section. If the bank has a dealer department, these procedures should not be performed. Applicable sections of these procedures have been incorporated into the dealer bank procedures.

The following summary is provided to assist the examiner in comprehending the repurchase agreement requirements of the Government Securities Act regulations.

Pooling of Securities

The regulations do not permit pooling of securities that are subject to repurchase transactions. Pooled repurchase transactions occur when a dealer does not identify specific securities as belonging to specific counterparties.

Instead, the dealer sets aside or otherwise designates a pool of securities to collateralize its outstanding repurchase transactions. The main concern with pool repurchase transactions is whether they effectively convey an enforceable security interest to the counterparties to the transaction. Previous operational practice with these transactions has been to issue a confirmation that referred only to "various securities." The regulations require that a dealer confirm specific securities to its counterparty in a hold-in-custody transaction. (17 CFR 403.5(d)(1)(ii))

Required Repurchase Agreement Disclosure

When the bank has been granted the right to substitute securities in repurchase transactions, the following disclosure must be included in the written repurchase agreement immediately preceding the provision governing the right to substitution:

"The (seller) is not permitted to substitute other securities for those subject to this agreement and therefore must keep the (buyer's) securities segregated at all times, unless in this agreement the (buyer) grants the (seller) the right to substitute other securities. If the (buyer) grants the right to substitute, this means that the (buyer's) securities will likely be commingled with the (seller's) own securities during the trading day. The (buyer) is advised that, during any trading day that the (buyer's) securities are commingled with the (seller's) securities, they may be subject to liens granted by the (seller) to third parties and may be used by the (seller) for deliveries on other securities transactions. Whenever the securities are commingled, the (seller's) ability to resegregate substitute securities for the (buyer) will be subject to the (seller's) ability to satisfy any lien or to obtain substitute securities."

Confirmation Tickets for Repurchase Agreements

If the bank retains custody of securities or retains the right to substitute securities during a repurchase agreement, it must identify in writing the specific securities that are collateralizing the repurchase agreement. This identification is satisfied by providing the counterparty with a confirmation ticket at the end of day the transaction is initiated. An additional confirmation ticket must be sent out at the end of each day that other securities are substituted by the bank during the repurchase agreement. Only the security involved in the last substitution of the day must be disclosed on the confirmation ticket (17 CFR 403.5(d)(1)(ii)). The confirmation ticket must specify at a minimum the issuer of the security, maturity date, coupon rate, par amount and market value of the security, and the CUSIP or mortgage pool number of the underlying security (17 CFR 403.5(d)(2)(i))

Tier I Procedures

Board of Director's Supervision

1. Assess the adequacy of written policies established by the board of directors or a designated committee. Determine whether the policies:

   a. Address "hold-in-custody" repurchase transactions.

   b. Address custodial holdings of customer securities.

   c. Establish guidelines for securities lending activities that comply with Banking Circular 196.

2. Determine whether the board or a designated committee review the policies for adequacy at least annually.

3. Ascertain whether the board or a designated committee ensures that the bank is complying with its policies.

4. Determine whether possible violations of law, rules, and regulations are referred to legal counsel for review, and if so, whether counsel submits written opinions to the board or a committee.

Management Supervision

5. Determine management's commitment to correcting matters cited in reports of examination. If matters have not been corrected, determine why not.

6. Ascertain whether all violations, possible violations, or deficiencies that have been reported to the board or a designated committee by either the audit or compliance staffs have been corrected or addressed adequately.

Compliance Management

7. Determine if the bank has established a written compliance policy.

8. If so, determine whether the policy requires compliance testing by asking the following questions:

   a. How frequently?

   b. To what extent?

9. Ascertain whether a person(s) is responsible for compliance with applicable rules, laws, and regulations and whether:

   a. The person is independent.

   b. The person is qualified (based on training and experience) to effectively monitor the assigned areas.

   c. The person performs periodic (at least annual) reviews of the bank's activities (custody of customer securities and "hold-in-custody" repos, etc.).

   d. Such reviews are conducted pursuant to written compliance testing procedures.

10. Assess whether the person responsible for compliance submits a written report to the board or designated committee at least annually.

11. Evaluate whether the scope of the compliance review is sufficient to review compliance with applicable sections of the Government Securities Act of 1986 and Banking Circulars 196 and 210.

Audit

12. Assess whether the bank's audit staff (either internal or holding company) periodically reviews the bank's activities, including a review for compliance with applicable rules and regulations, and whether:

    a. The audit staff is independent and qualified to review the bank's activities.

b. The review is conducted at least annually.

c. The review is conducted pursuant to comprehensive written audit policies and procedures.

Investor Protection

Custody of Customer-Owned Securities (17 CFR 403.5)

13. Ascertain whether the bank has established adequate written procedures and internal controls to determine, on each business day, the quantity and issue of such securities, if any, that are required to be but are not in the financial institution's possession or control. (17 CFR 403.5(c)(2))

14. Determine whether the procedures address:

a. Releases of liens, charges, or encumbrances against affected securities.

b. Returns of securities loaned.

c. Steps to obtain possession or control of securities failed to receive for more than 30 days (except for mortgage-backed securities).

d. "Buying in" securities as necessary when securities shortages in possession or control cannot be resolved by any of the preceding procedures.

NOTE: The procedures detailed in step 14 are the minimum required by the regulation. If any of them are excluded, the bank is in violation of the regulation.

Repurchase Agreements (Hold-In-Custody Repos)

15. If the bank retains custody of securities that are the subject of a repurchase transaction or if the bank retains custody of such securities, whether or not in safekeeping, and retains the right to substitute other securities for such securities, determine whether:

a. The bank ensures that repurchase agreements are in written form, and if so, whether the written repurchase agreement explicitly advises the counterparty that funds held by the bank pursuant to the repurchase agreement are not a deposit and therefore not insured by the FDIC.

b. The bank confirms in writing, at the end of the trading day on which the transaction occurred, the specific securities which are the subject of the transaction.

c. The bank maintains possession or control of securities that are the subject of the agreement. (17 CFR 403.5(d)(1)(vi))

d. The bank substitutes collateral resulting in a change in issuer, maturity date, par amount, or coupon rate.

e. If the bank substitutes collateral:

- The bank's right to substitute securities and proper disclosure to the counterparty is included in the written repurchase agreement. (17 CFR 403.5(d)(1)(v))

- The substitution is confirmed in writing with the counterparty at the end of the trading day on which the substitution occurs. (17 CFR 403.5(d)(1)(i))

- The written confirmation provides the customer with adequate disclosure. (17 CFR 403.5(d)(2)(i)) (Refer to the introduction for minimum requirements.)

"Due Bills"

16. Ascertain whether the bank has accepted customer funds for securities purchases, but has not placed the order by the close of the next business day after receipt:

a. The bank immediately deposits or redeposits the funds in the customer's account and sends the customer notice of such deposit and redeposit.

b. If not, the bank complies with the "buy-in" provisions of the regulations.

17. Determine if the bank complies with Banking Circular 182 when issuing

"due bills" to customers.

Custodial Holdings of Government Securities (17 CFR 450)

The bank is exempt from the requirements of Section 450 if the responses to questions 18 and 19 are yes (17 CFR 450.3). If the bank maintains custody of securities not subject to examination for compliance with 12 CFR 9 (e.g., commercial bank safekeeping), the bank must comply with Section 450.

Customer Holdings Subject to Fiduciary Standards

18.Determine whether the bank exercises fiduciary powers.

19.Ascertain if the bank's custodial holdings of government securities:

　a.　Are administered pursuant to written policies and procedures that apply all the applicable requirements imposed by the OCC on fiduciary holdings of government securities.

　b.　Are subject to examination by the OCC for compliance with such fiduciary requirements.

Customer-Owned Securities Maintained On-Site (17 CFR 450.4)

20.Determine whether, if the bank is not exempt and maintains custody of securities on its premises, government securities held for customers are segregated from the bank's assets and kept free from lien of any third party or the bank.

Customer-Owned Securities Maintained at a Third Party (17 CFR 450.4)

NOTE: The bank is not required to have a segregated account at the FED for customer-owned securities if the securities are segregated in the bank's records. (17 CFR 450.4)

21.Determine whether if the bank maintains customer-owned securities at a third party:

　a.　The bank has notified the third party institution that such securities are customer-owned securities.

b. The customer-owned securities are maintained in an account specifically designated for bank customers and which does not contain securities belonging to the bank.

c. The bank has instructed the third party to maintain such securities free from liens of the third party or any persons claiming through it.

d. If the customer-owned securities are maintained by the bank at the FED, any liens or claims granted to FED or any person claiming through the FED expressly exclude customer securities.

Recordkeeping for Custodial Holdings (17 CFR 450.4)

The following recordkeeping requirements do not apply to repurchase transactions (RPs). RPs are addressed in section 403.5(d). However, those requirements apply to all national banks that hold securities for the account of customers, not only dealer banks.

Recordkeeping

22. Determine whether the bank issues a safekeeping receipt or confirmation for each security held for customers.

23. Ascertain whether the safekeeping receipt or confirmation identifies the:

a. Issuer.

b. Maturity date.

c. Par amount.

d. Coupon rate.

24. Determine whether the bank's records of government securities held for customers are kept separate and distinct from other bank records.

25. Assess whether the bank's records:

a. Identify each customer.

b. Identify each government security held for each customer (or the amount of each issue issued in book-entry form).

c. Describe the customer's interest in the security.

d. Indicate all receipts and deliveries of securities, and receipts and disbursements of cash.

e. Include a copy of the safekeeping receipt or confirmation issued for each government security held.

26. Determine whether the bank's records provide for an adequate audit of recordkeeping information.

27. Assess whether the bank has established procedures to ensure that government securities held for customers in definitive and book entry form are counted at least annually and that such counts are also reconciled to customer account records.

NOTE: The regulations require that all government securities held for customers be counted annually. A sample is not acceptable.

28. Evaluate whether the bank's procedures include verifying securities:

a. In transfer.

b. In transit.

c. Pledged.

d. Loaned.

e. Borrowed.

f. Deposited.

g. Failed to receive.

h. Failed to deliver.

i. Subject to repurchase agreement.

j. Subject to reverse repurchase agreement.

k. Subject to the bank's control or direction, but not in its physical possession for longer than 30 days.

29. Determine whether the bank has developed procedures to document the dates and results of such counts and reconciliations and whether they are adequate.

30. Ascertain if differences are noted in a security count difference account not later than seven business days after the date of each required count and verification.

31. Determine if the bank has established procedures to comply with record retention requirements. (The requirements are the same as those for bank broker/dealer recordkeeping.)

Securities Lending — Customer-Owned Securities

Securities Lending Practices

32. Determine whether the bank lends customer-owned securities.

33. If the bank lends customer-owned securities, determine whether it obtained written authorization from the customer.

34. Determine whether securities lending activities fully comply with Banking Circular 196.

Repurchase Agreement Transactions

35. Determine whether the bank complies with Banking Circular 210, if it engages in repurchase transactions without retaining custody of customer securities.

NOTE: Banks that engage in those types of transactions are not subject to Government Securities Act requirements governing repurchase agreement transactions.

12 CFR 12 Recordkeeping and Confirmation Requirements

36. Determine whether the bank must comply with the recordkeeping and confirmation requirements of 12 CFR 12. Banks that handle an average of less than 200 securities transactions per year, over the previous three years, are exempt. The 200 transactions threshold excludes U.S. government and federal agency obligations.

Conclusions

37. Summarize in a memorandum the results of the supervisory review, addressing:

    a. Department management.

    b. Compliance management.

    c. Compliance with law.

    d. Internal audit.

    e. Condition of the department.

    f. Future prospects.

38. Results of the supervisory review, including violations of laws, rules, regulations, or significant deficiencies, and management response should be discussed in the examination report provided to the board of directors. The causes of such violations or deficiencies should be emphasized. Violations and significant deficiencies found by the examiner and by internal audit and/or compliance management that remain uncorrected should be commented upon.

www.ingramcontent.com/pod-product-compliance
Lightning Source LLC
Chambersburg PA
CBHW080517290526
45790CB00006B/2201